name ....

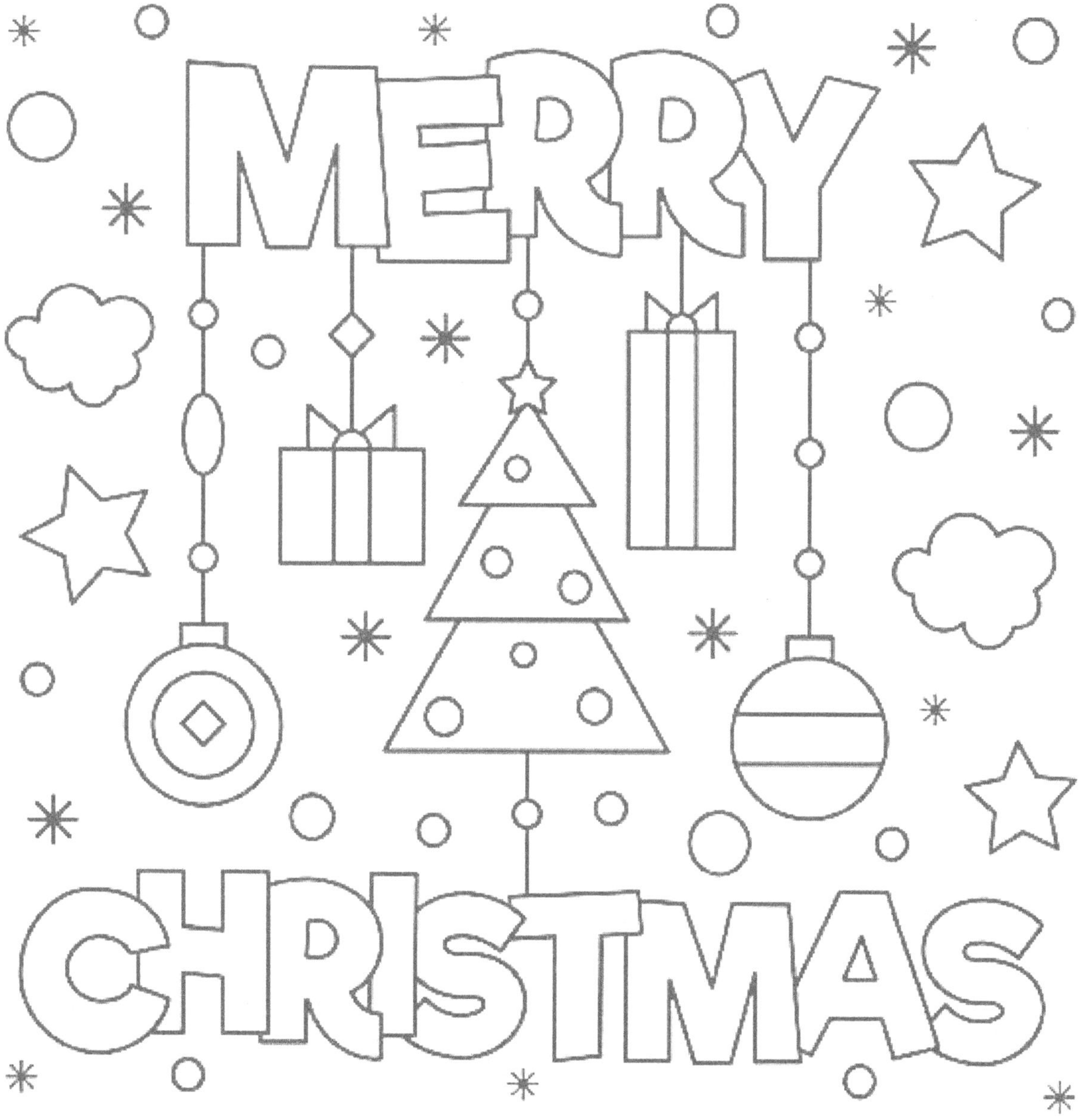

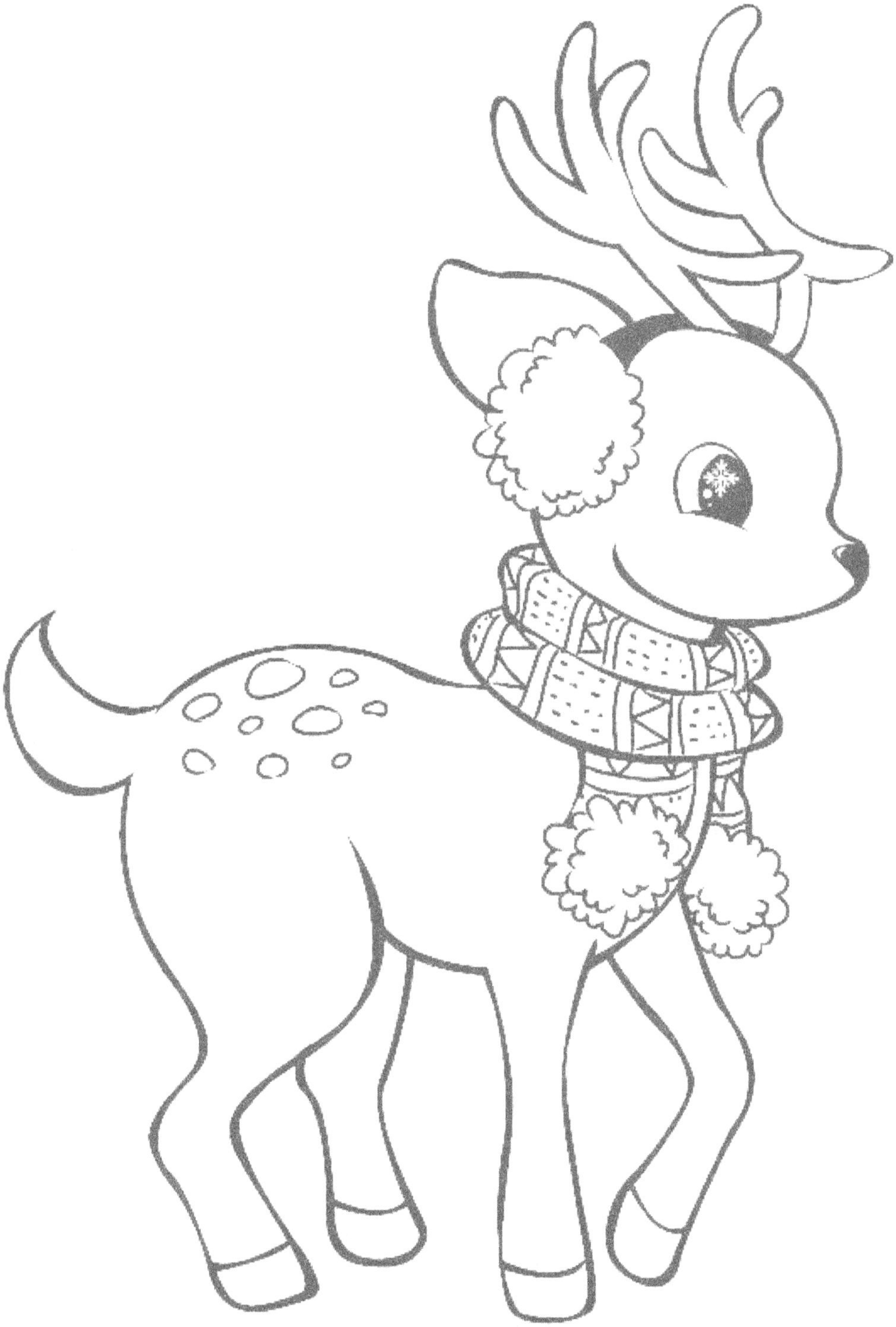

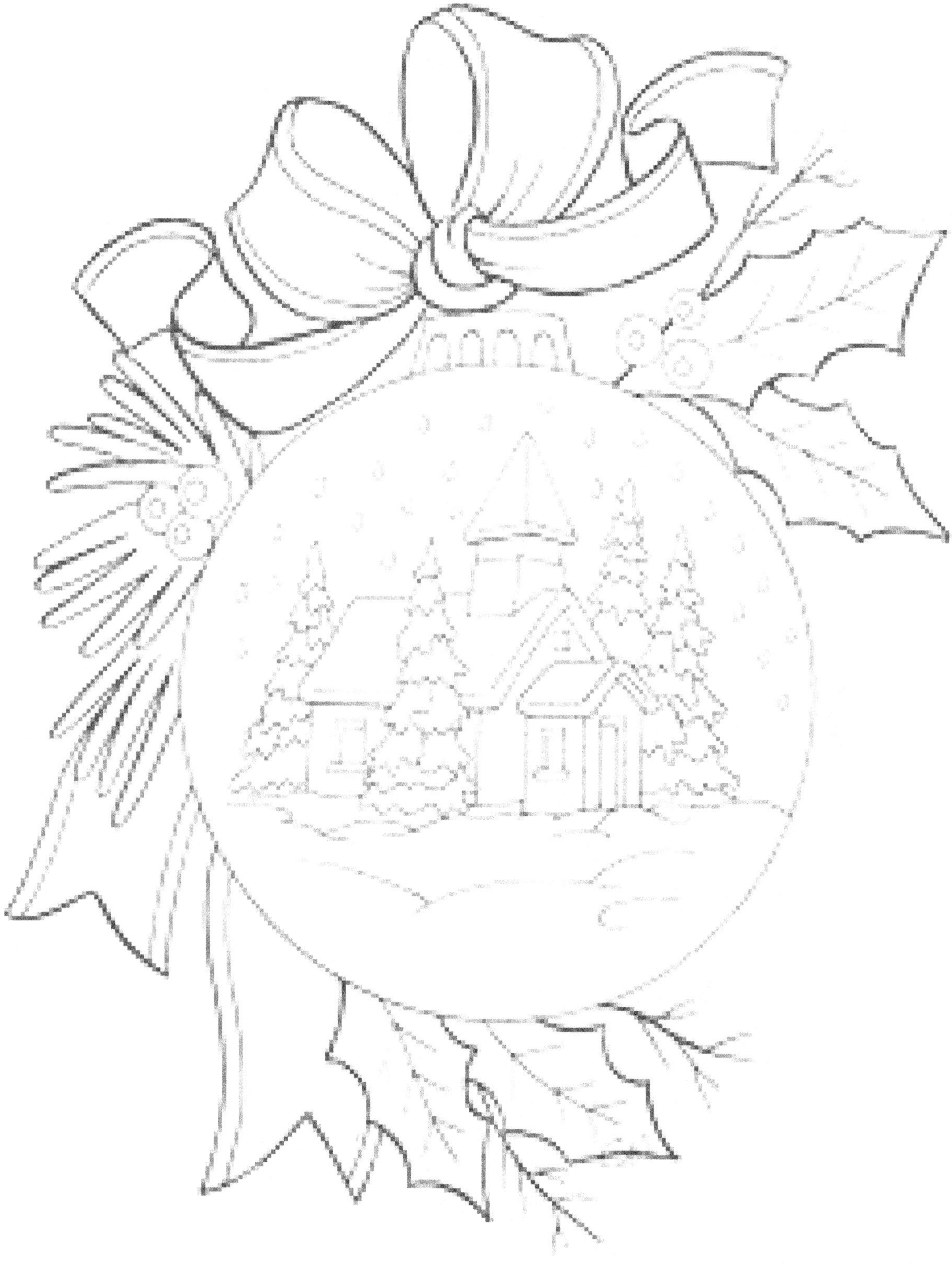

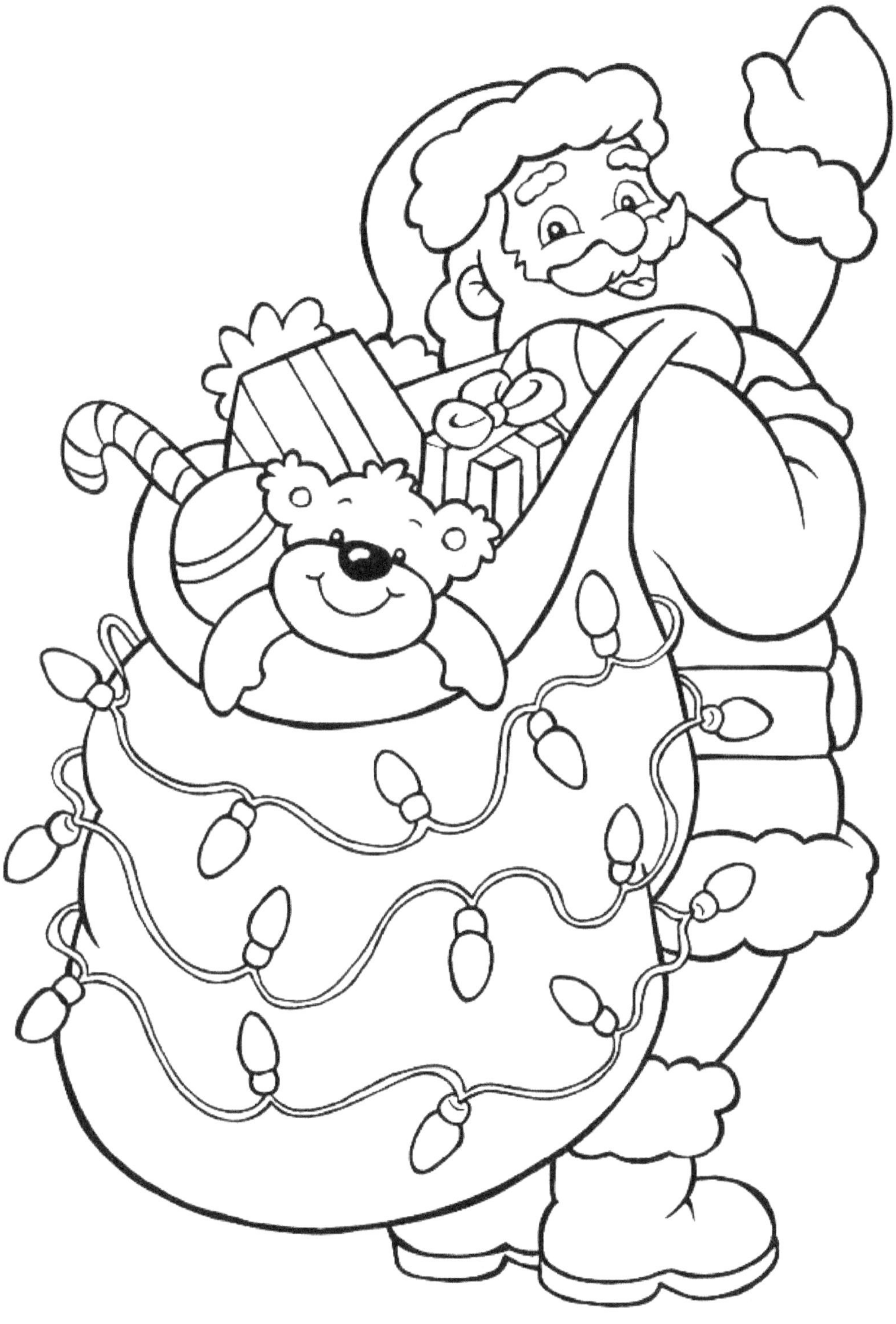

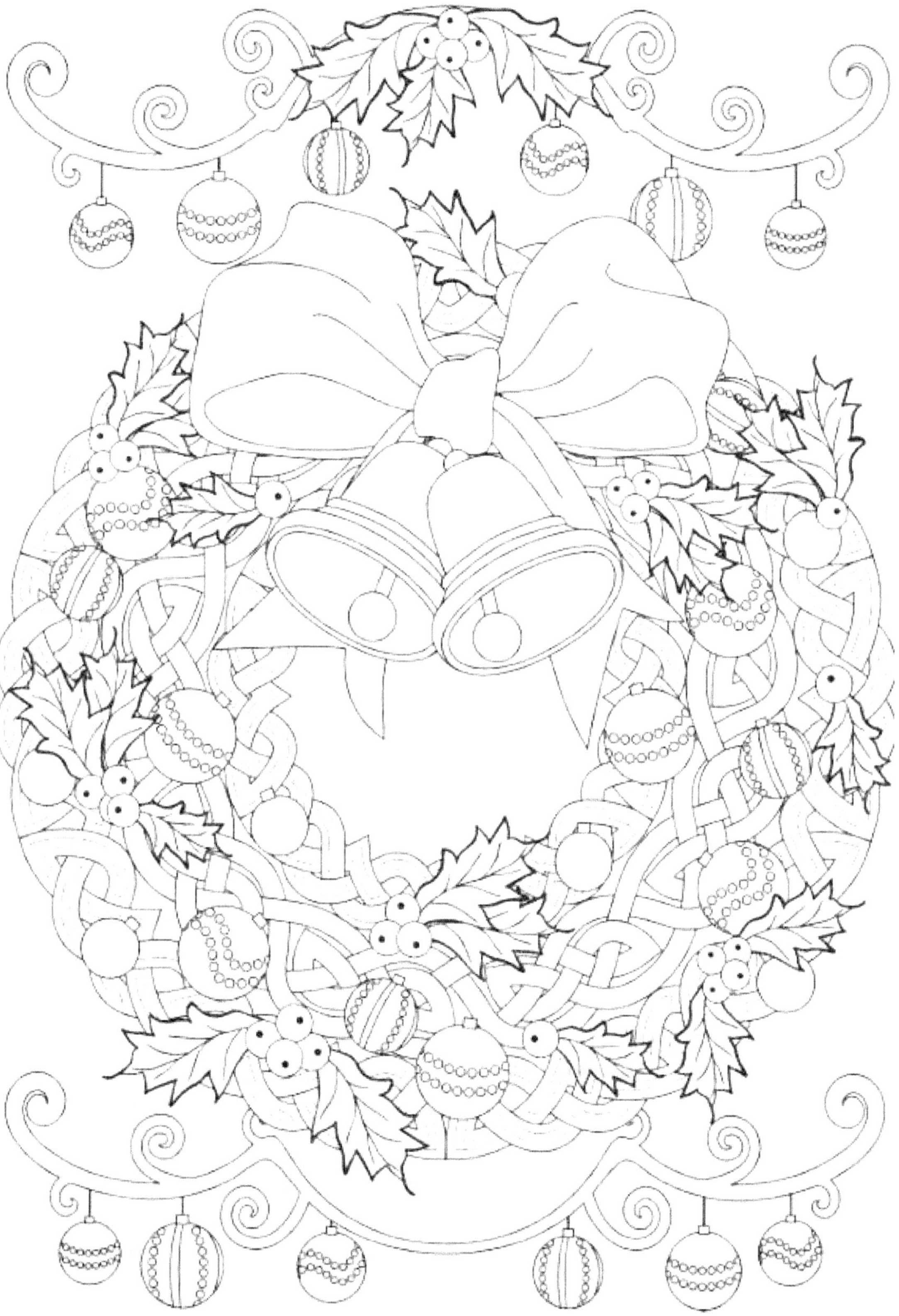

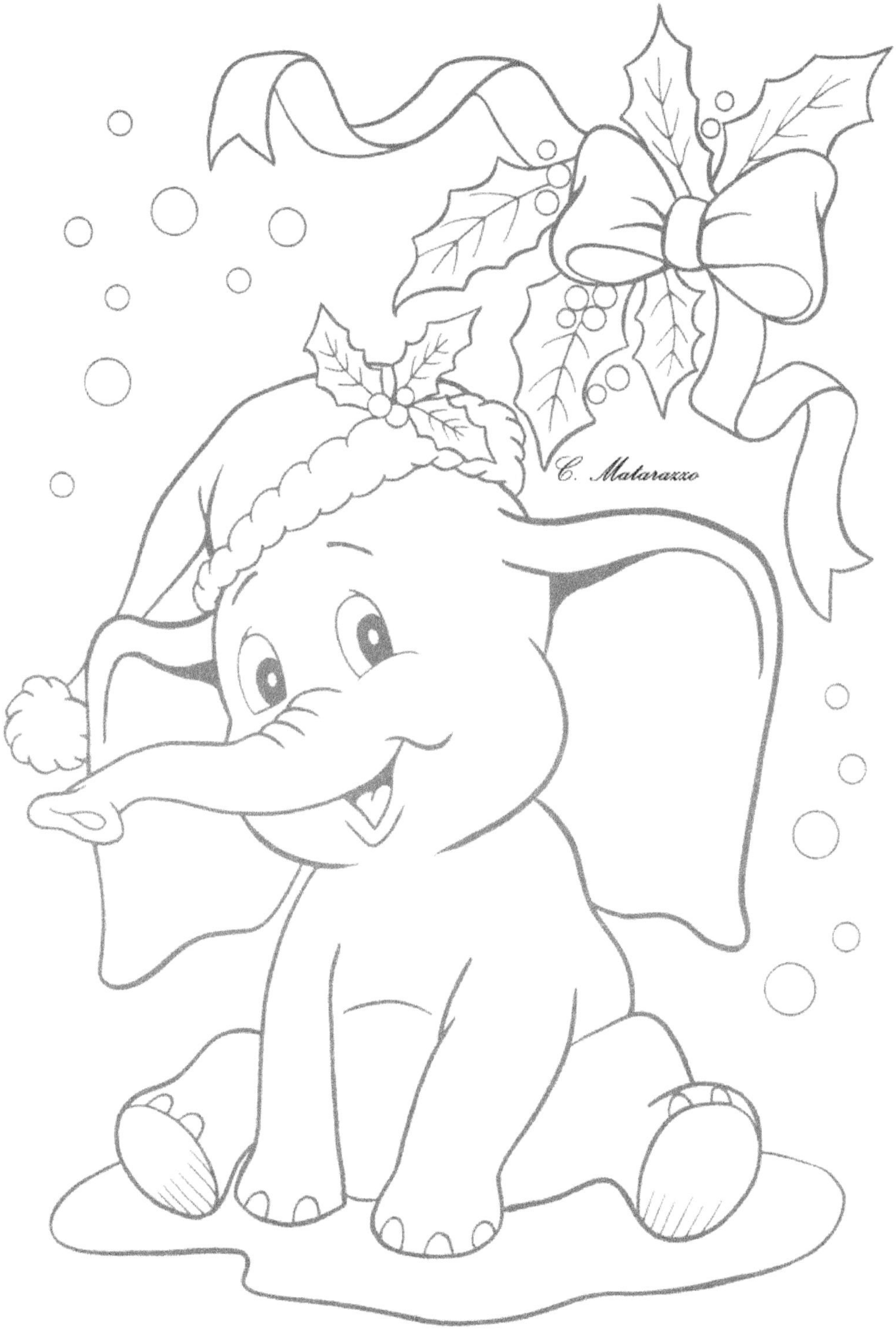
C. Matarazzo

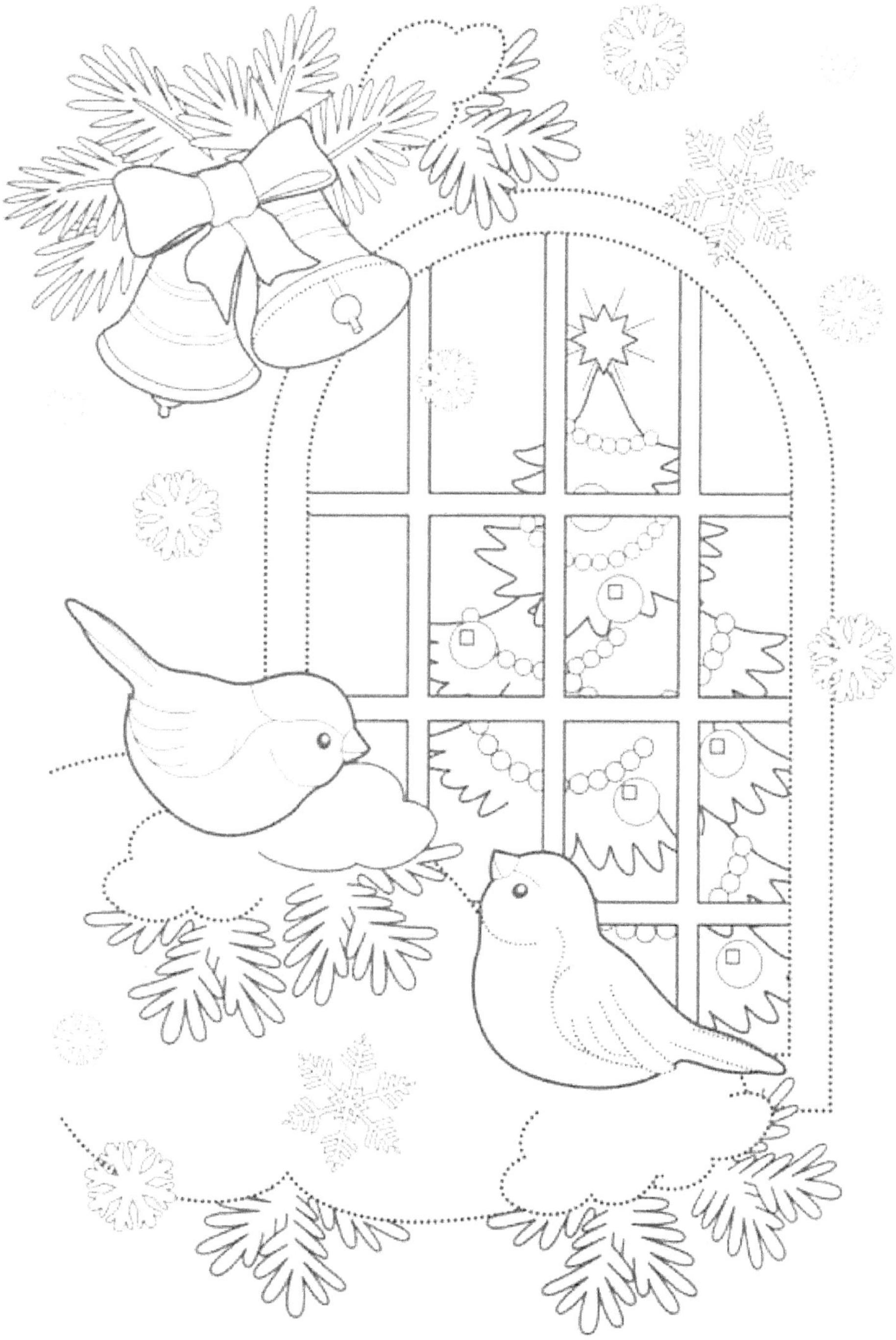

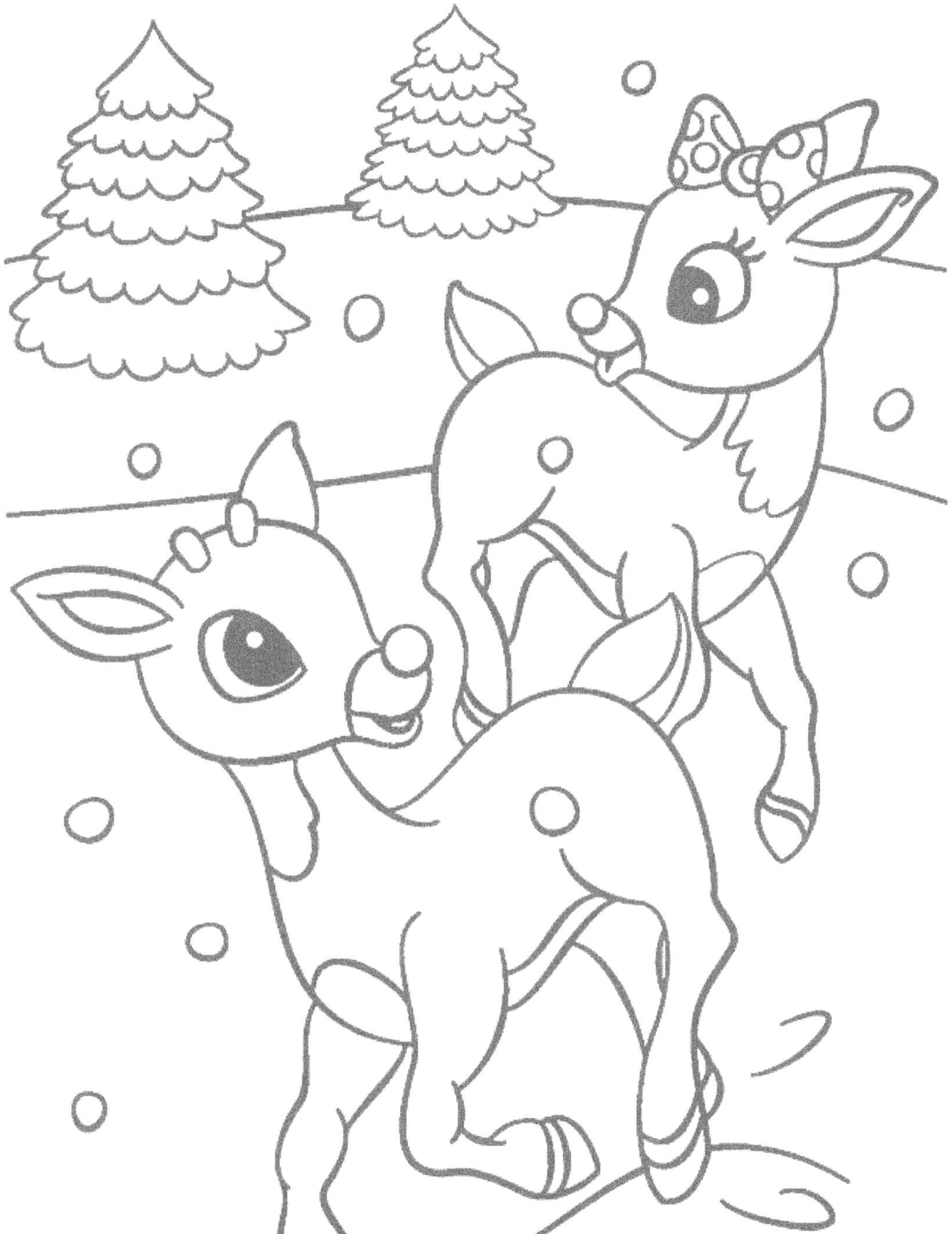

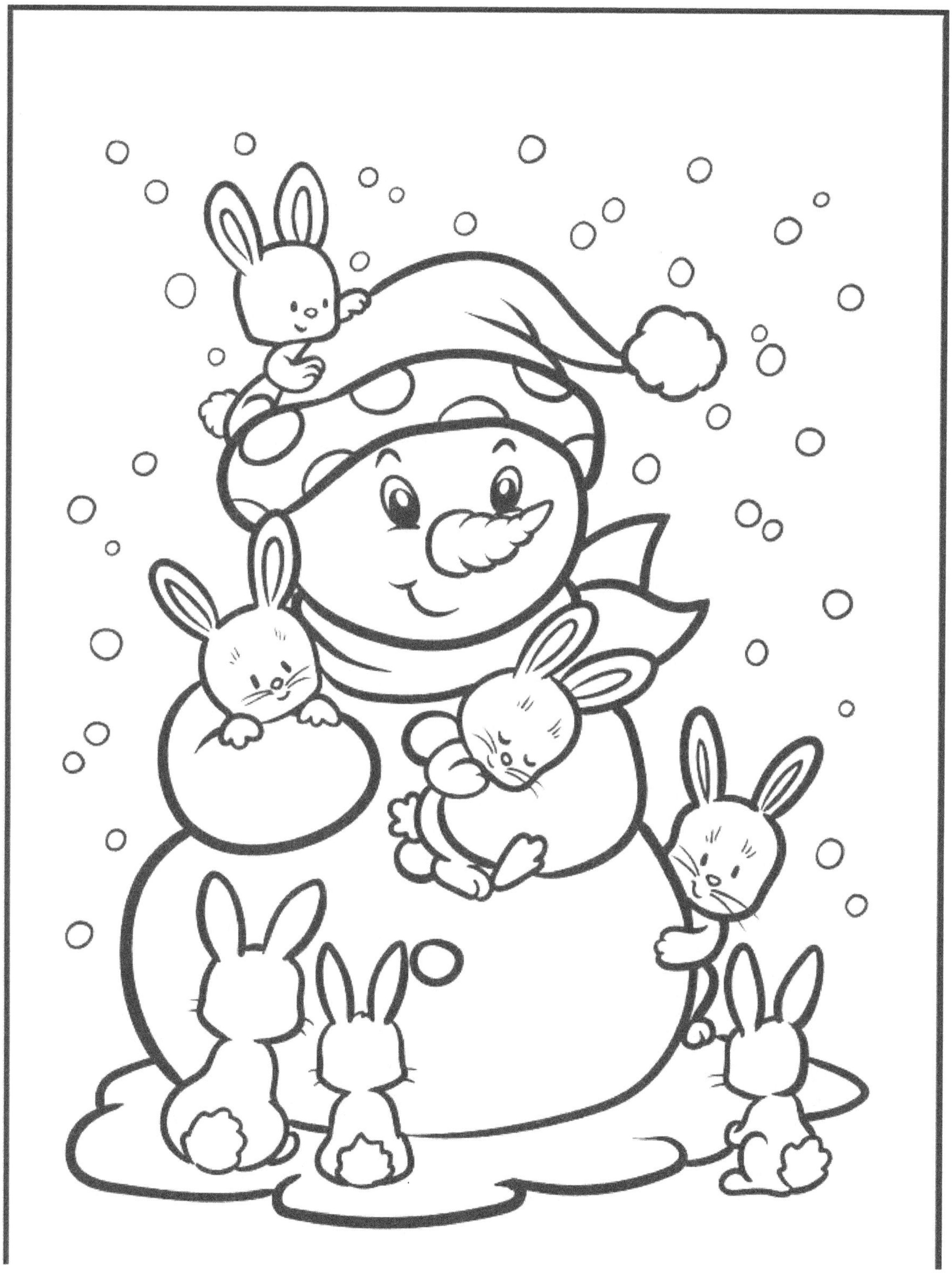

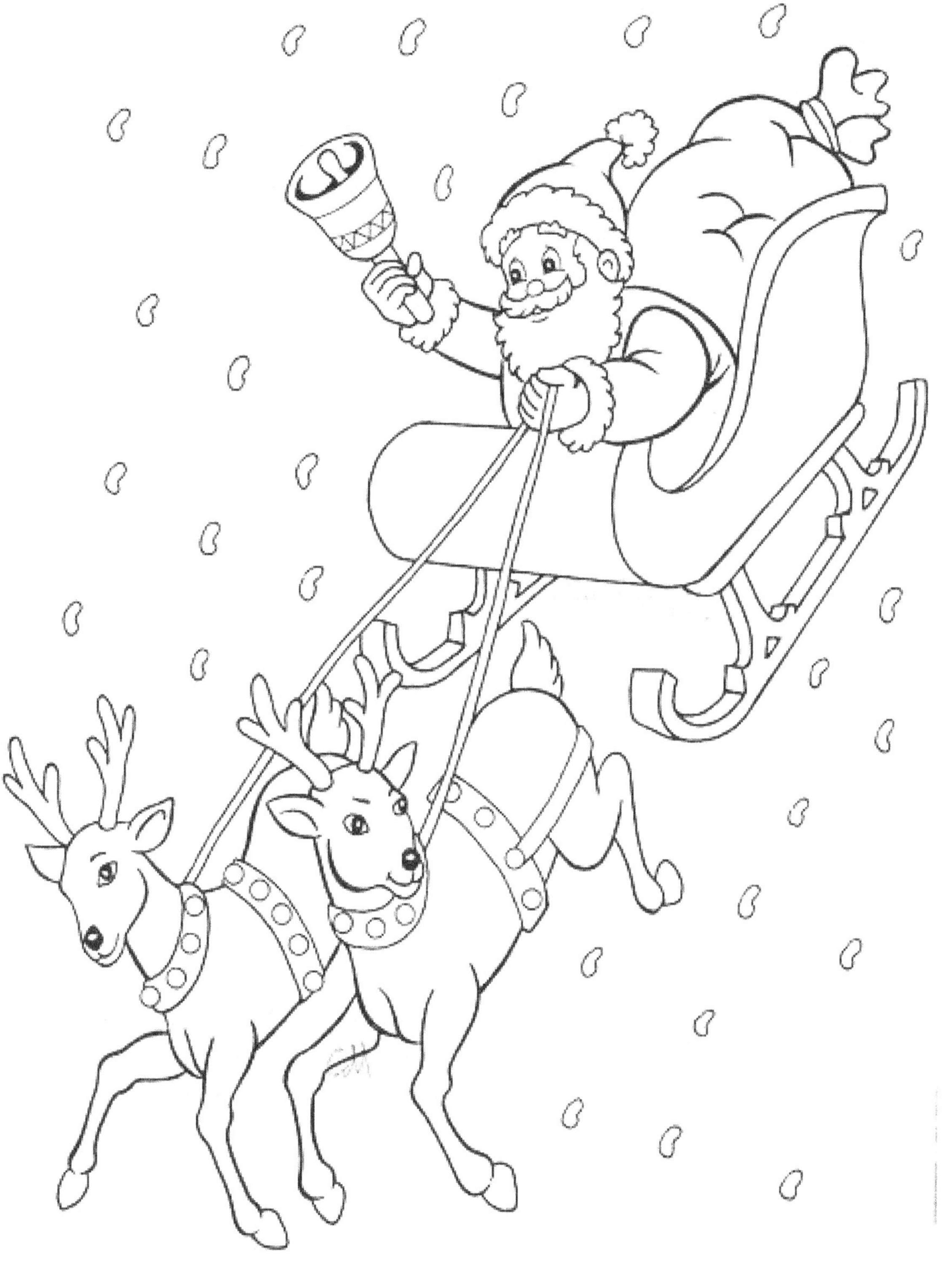

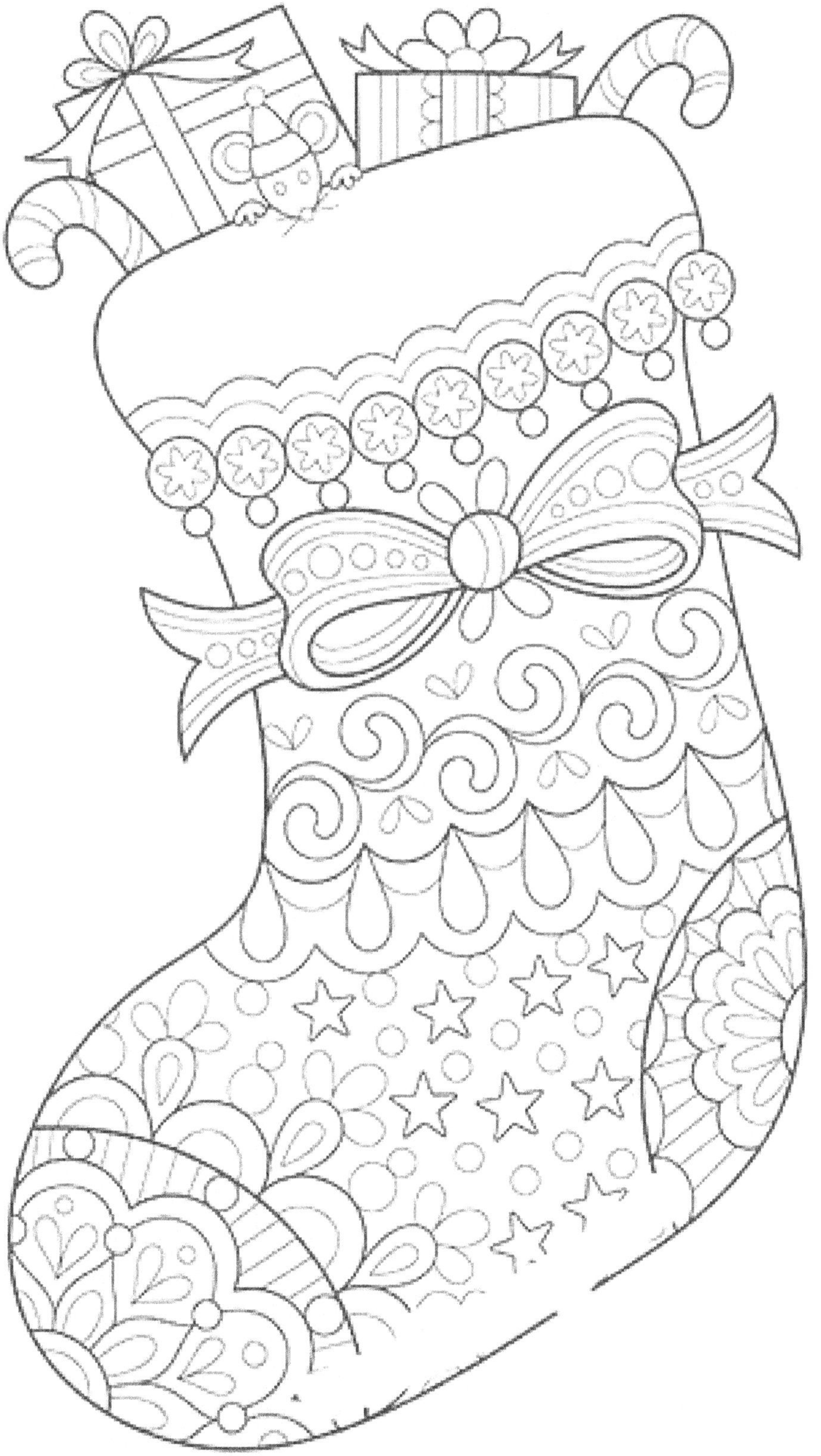

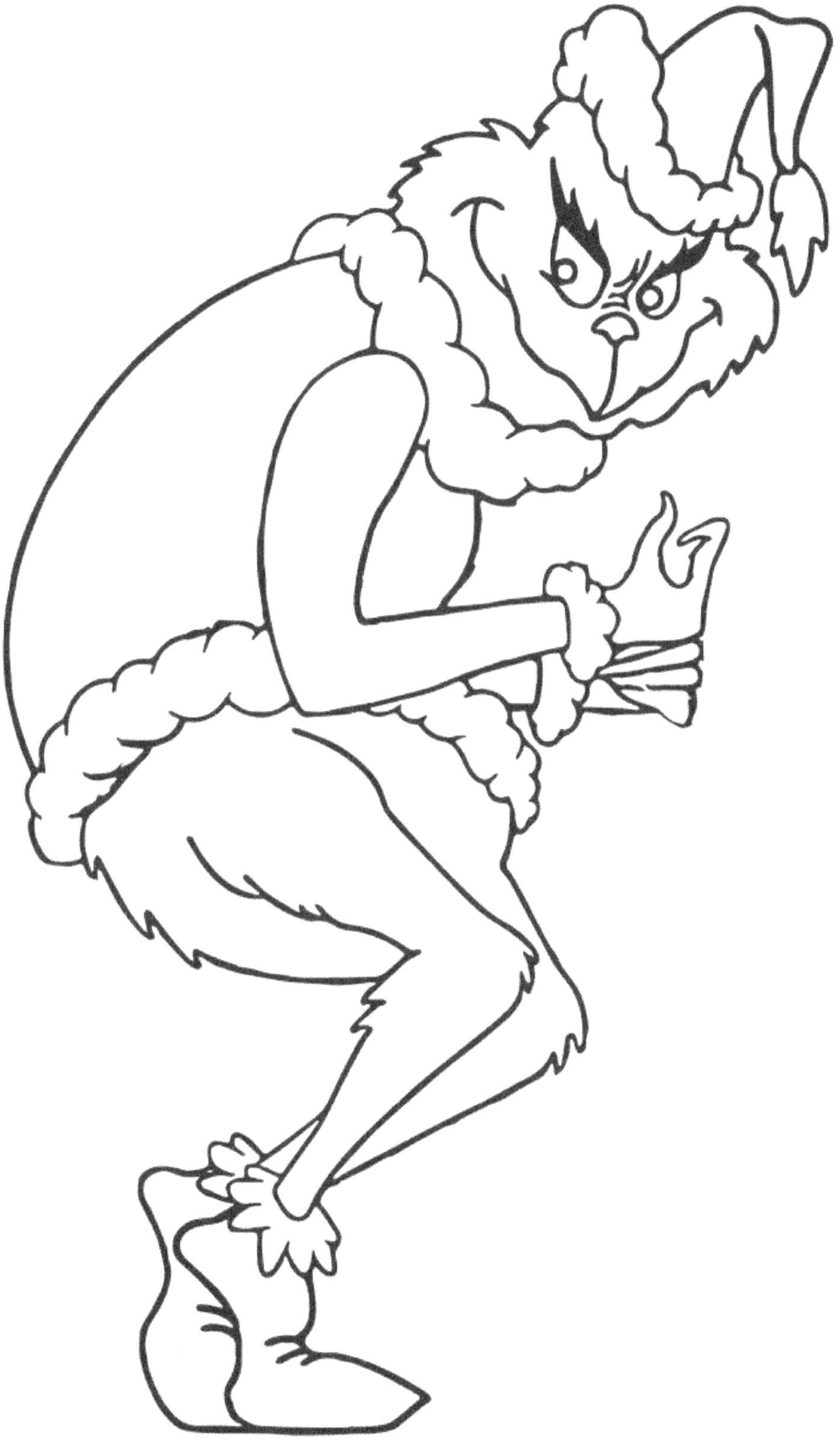

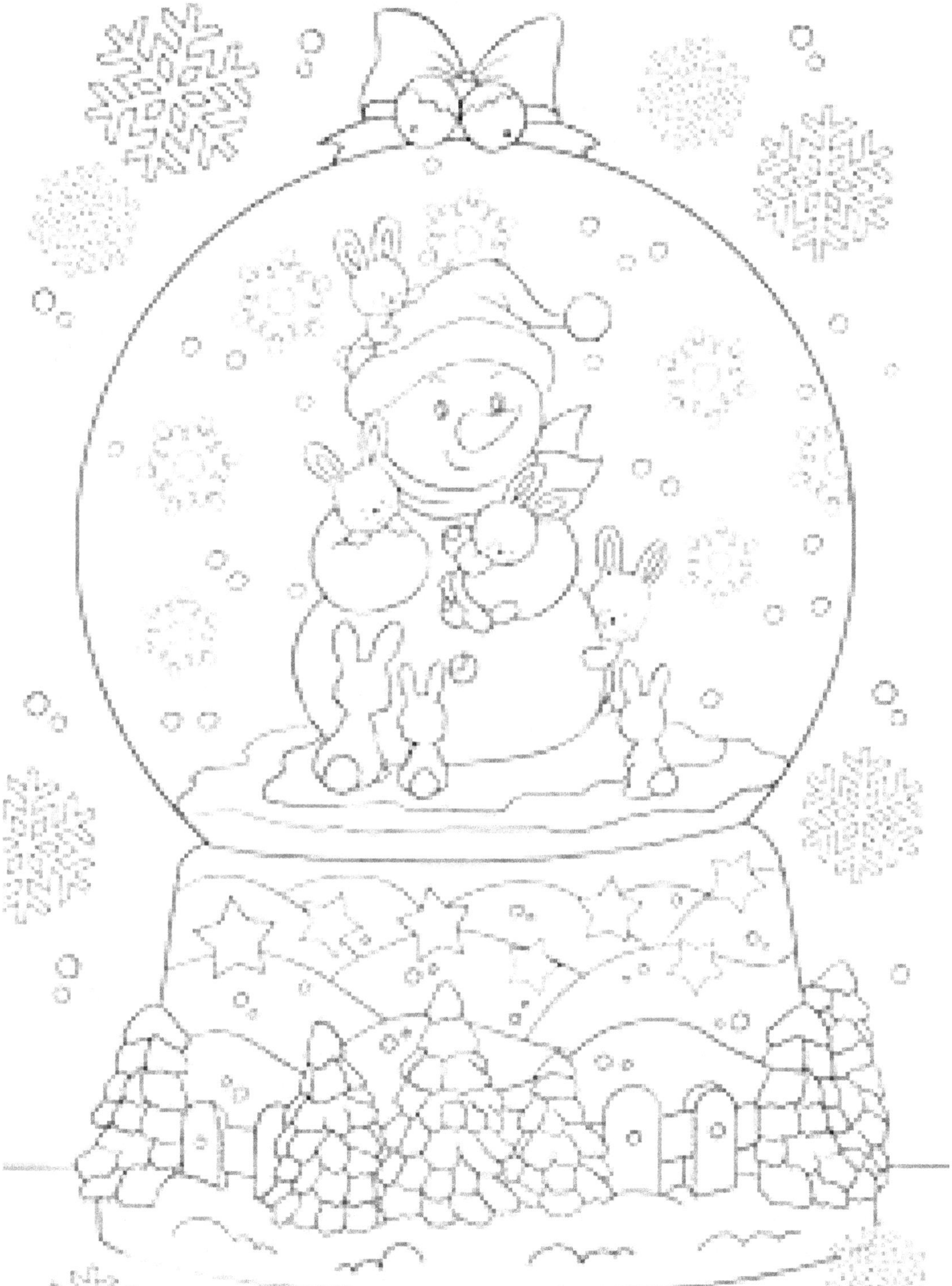

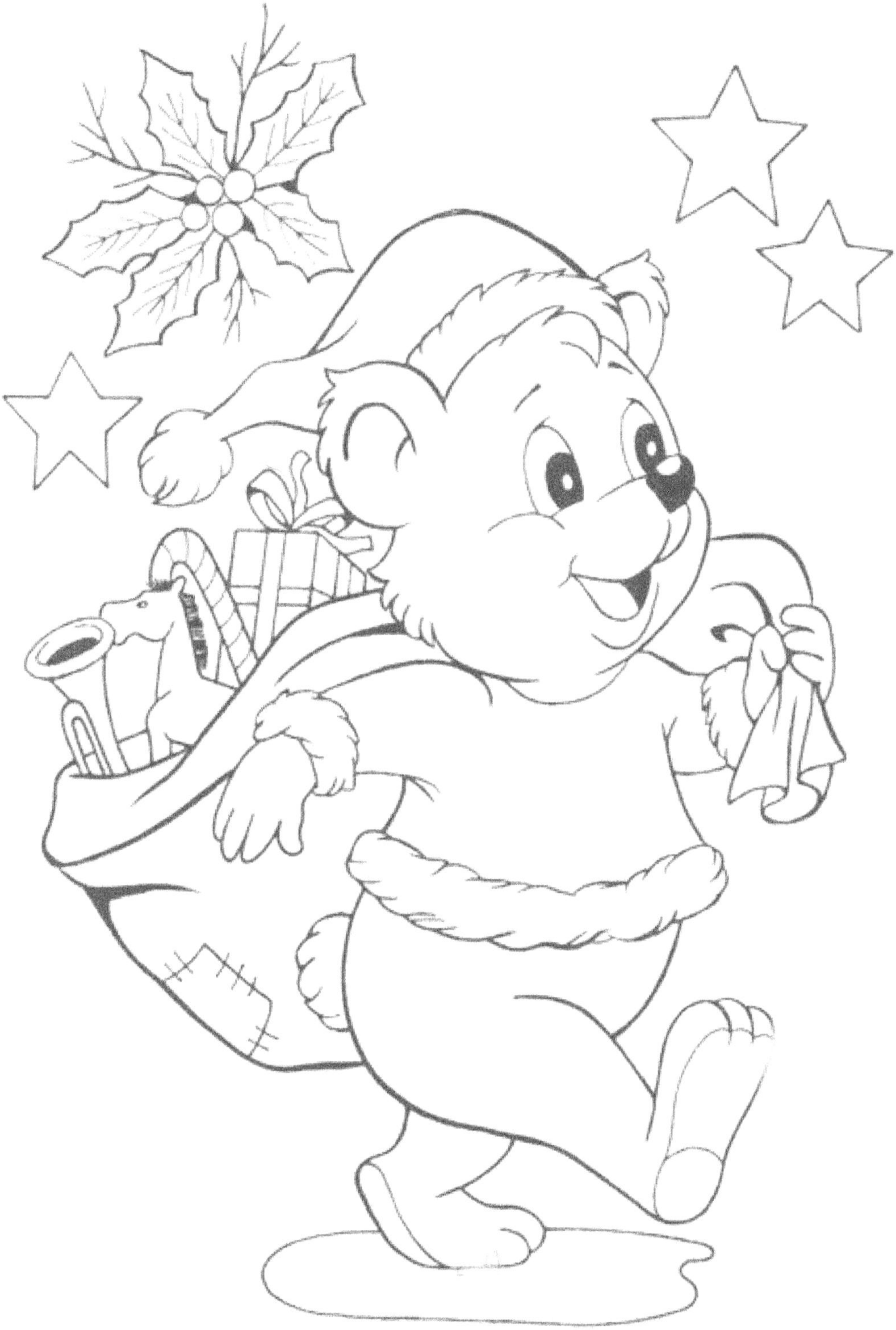

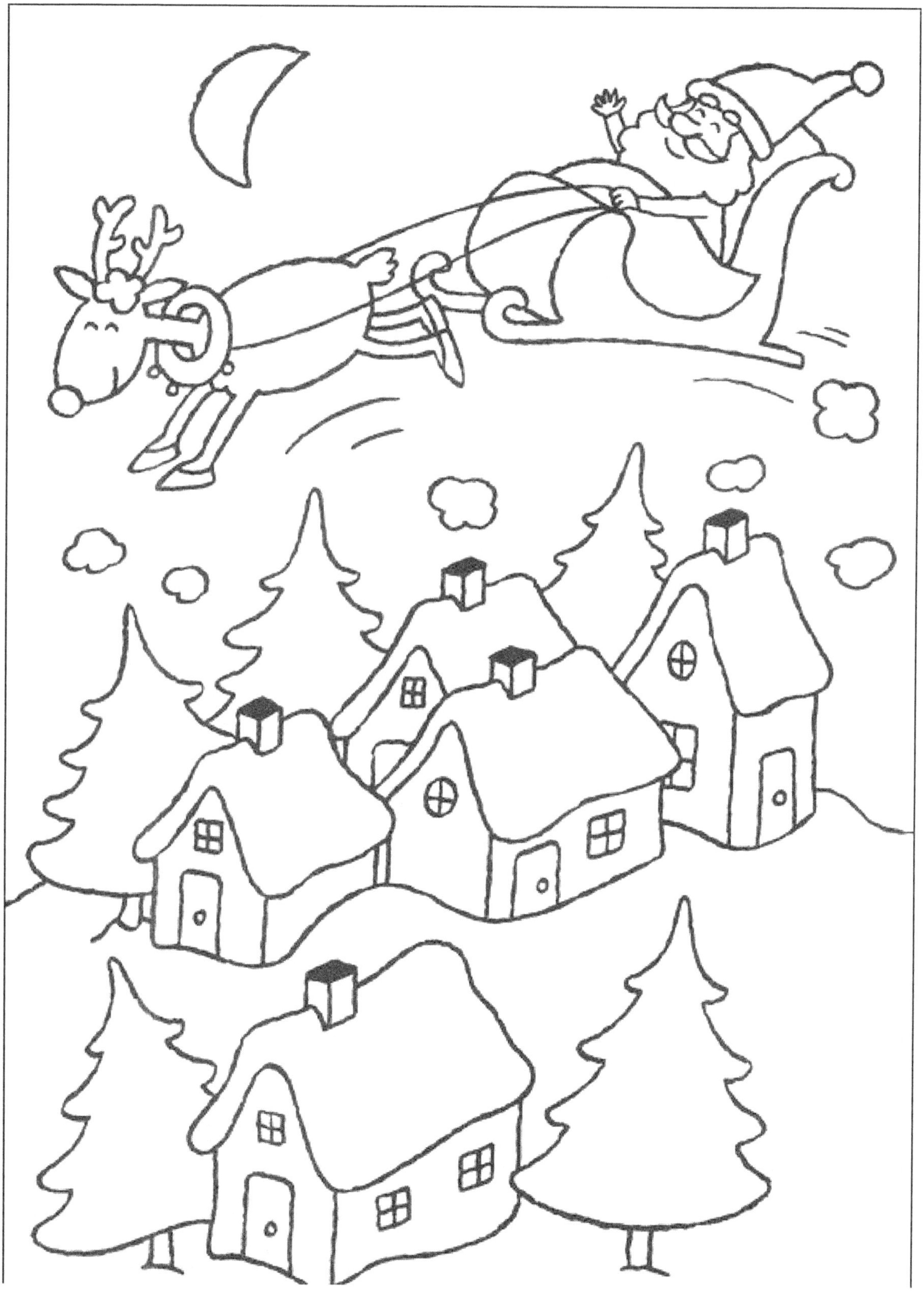

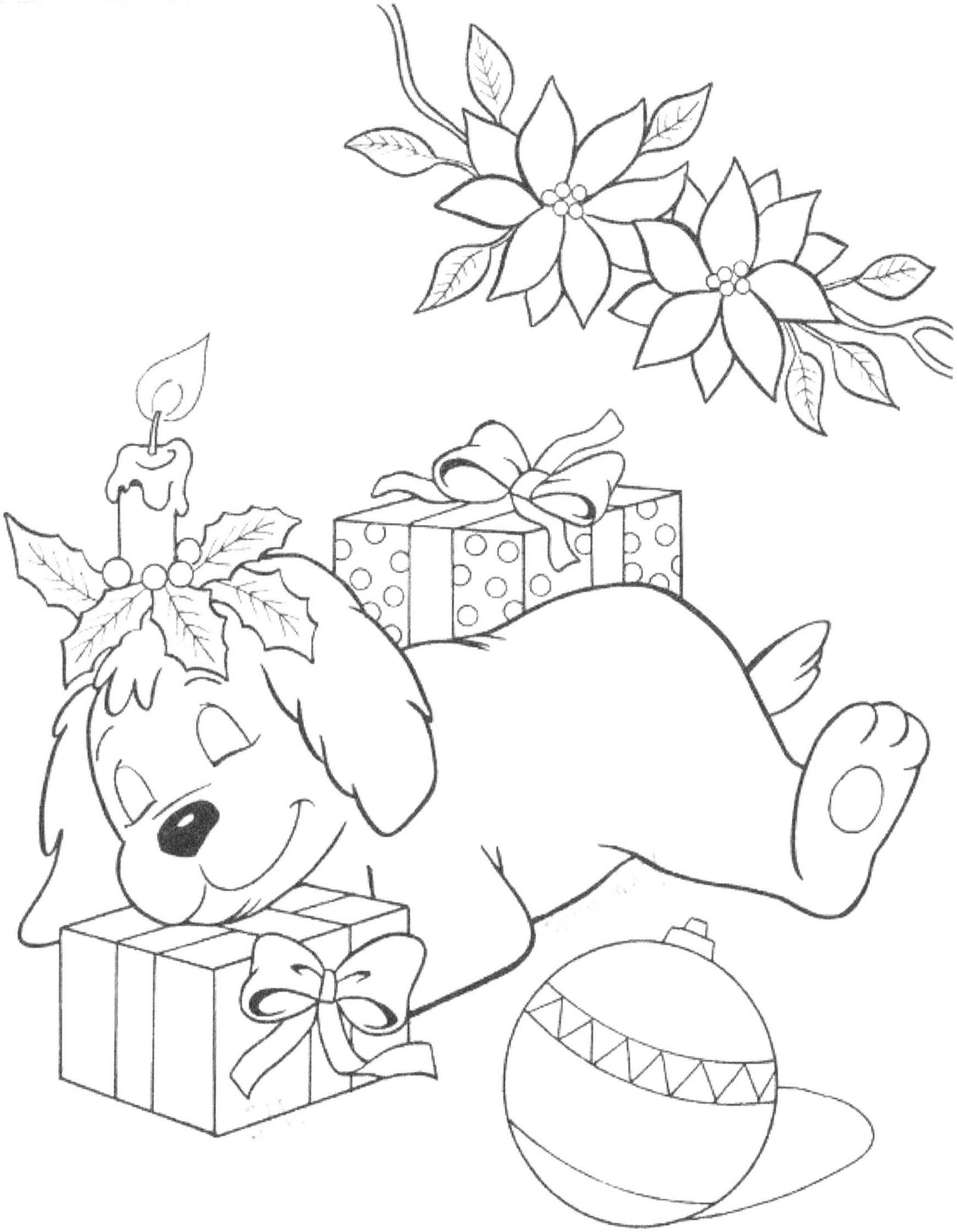

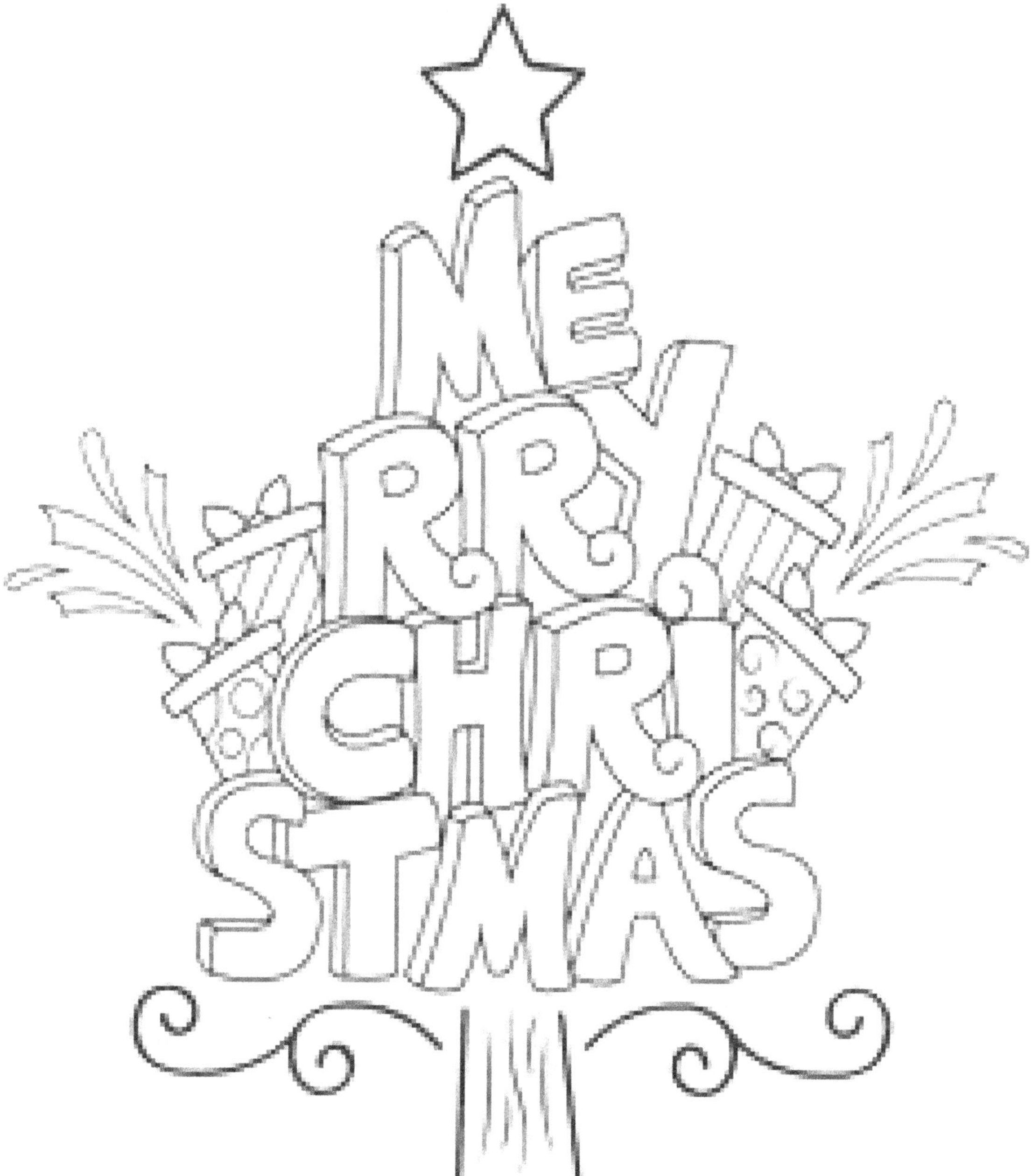
MERRY
CHRISTMAS

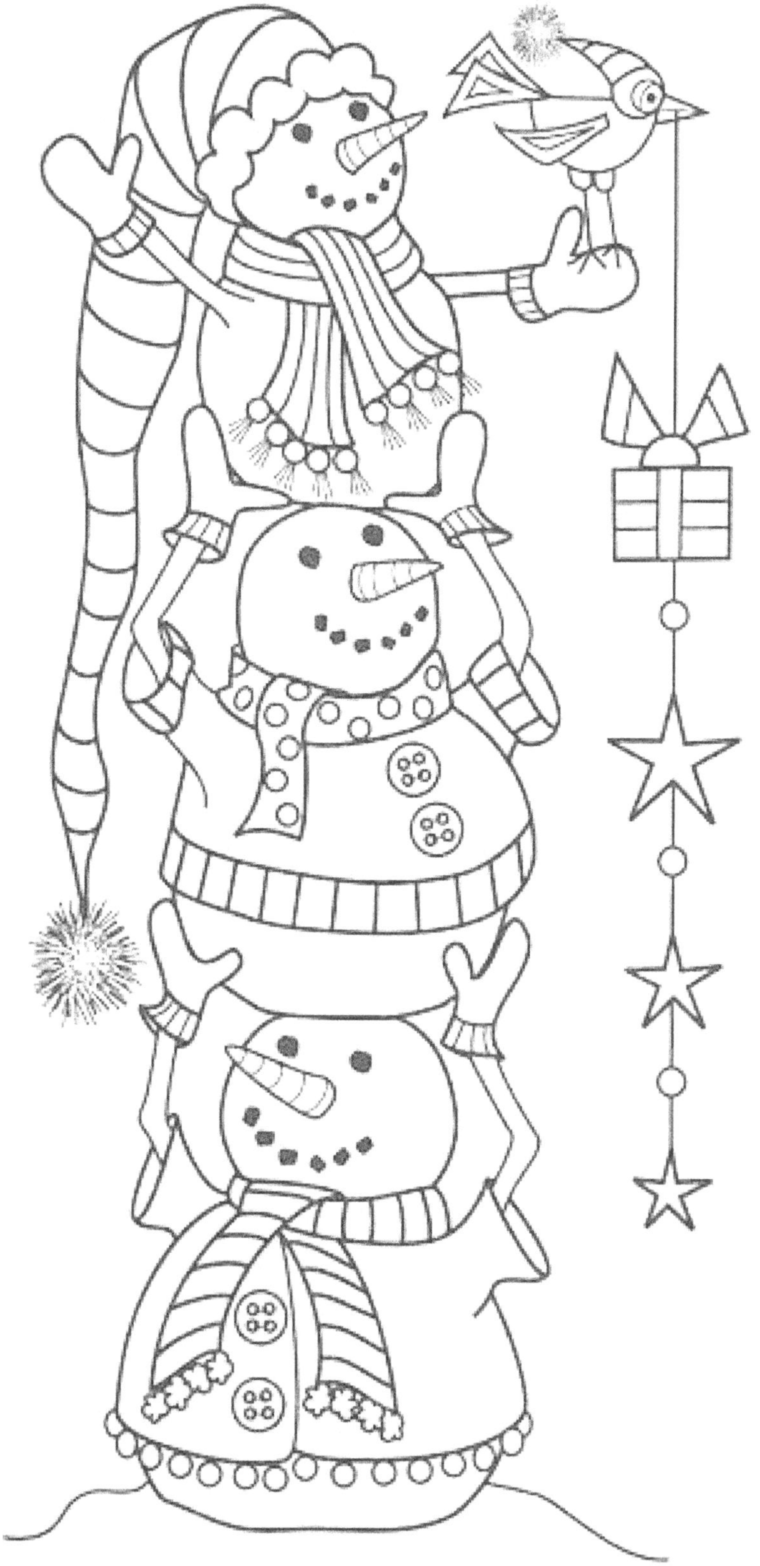

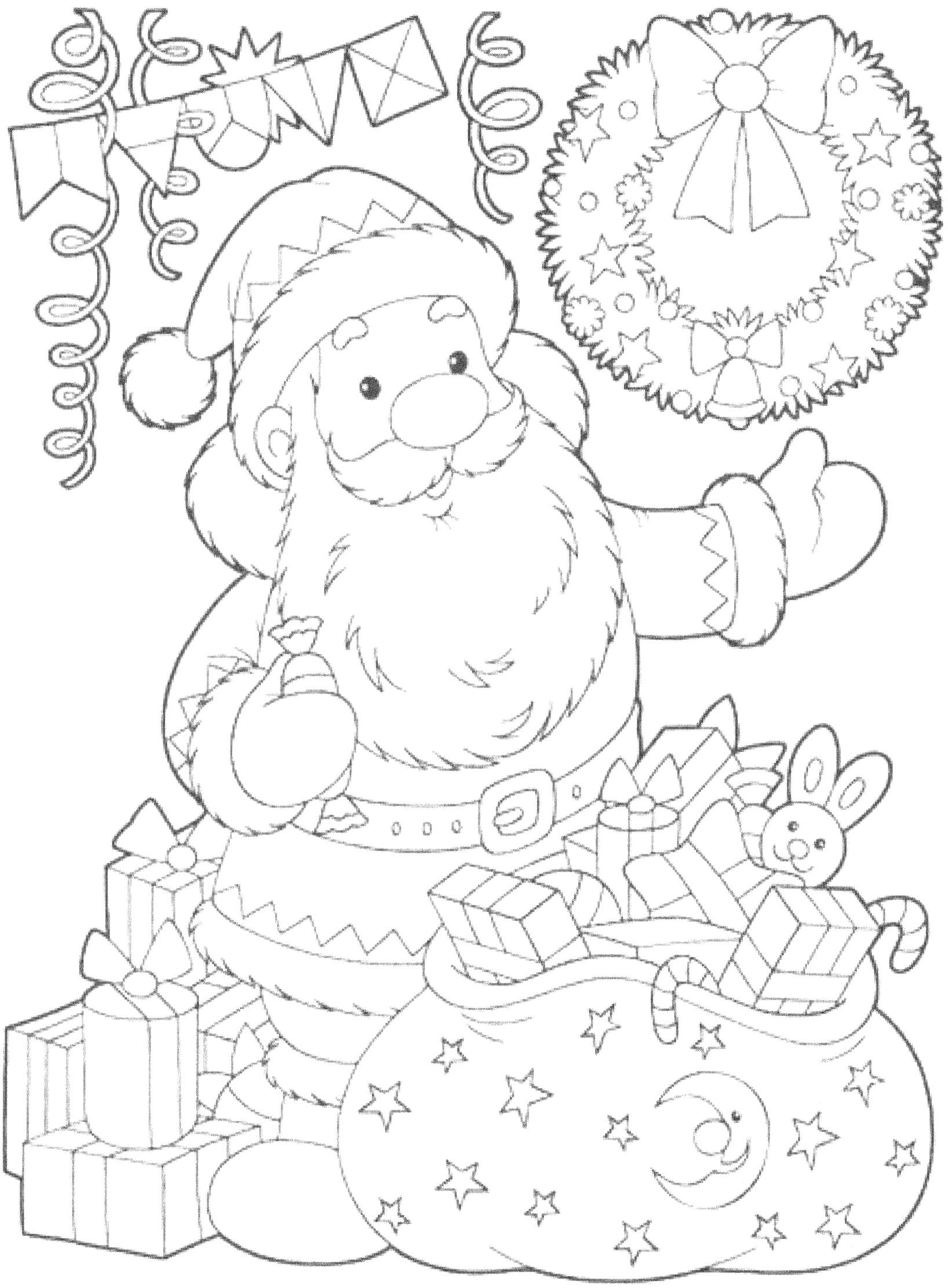

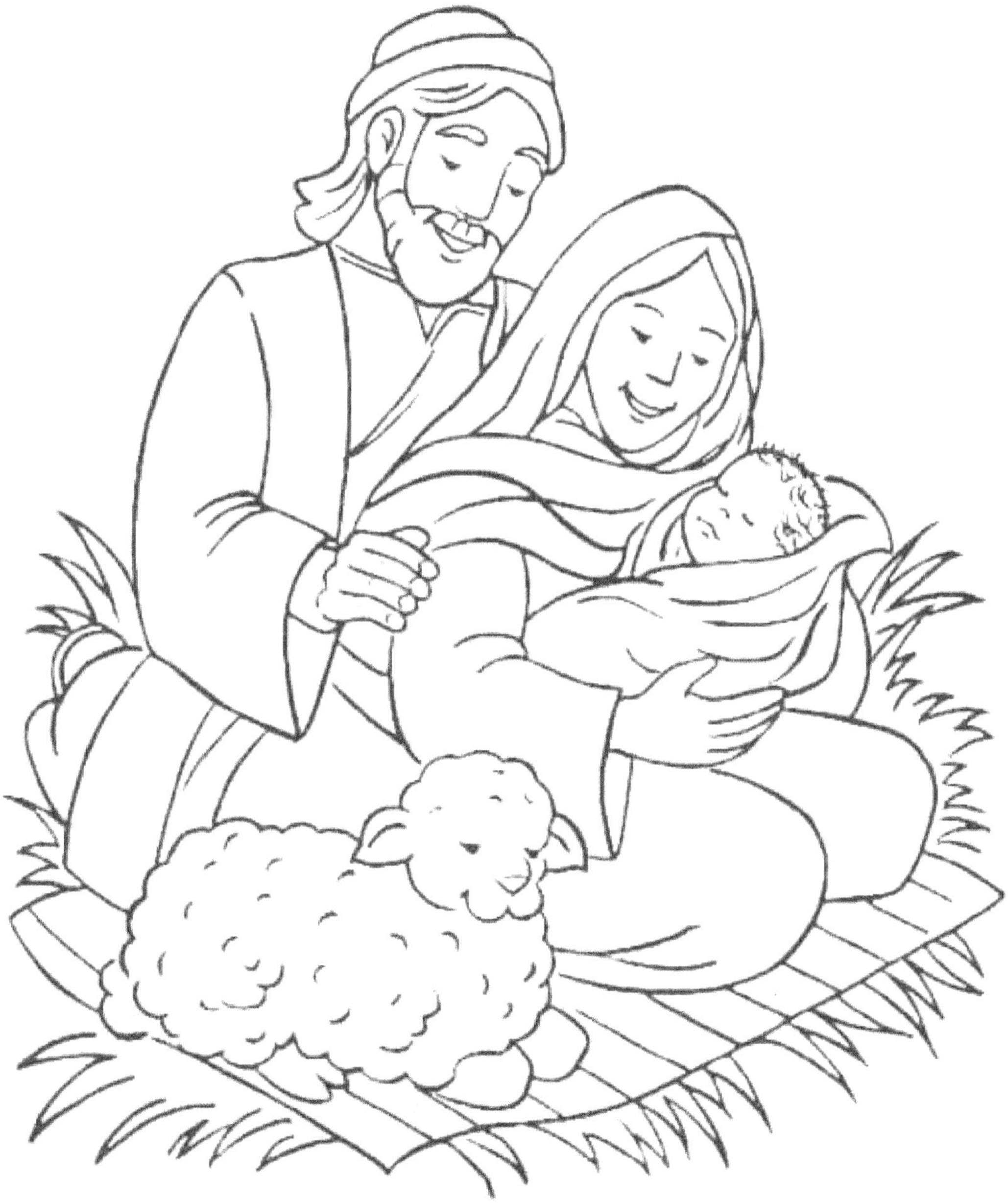

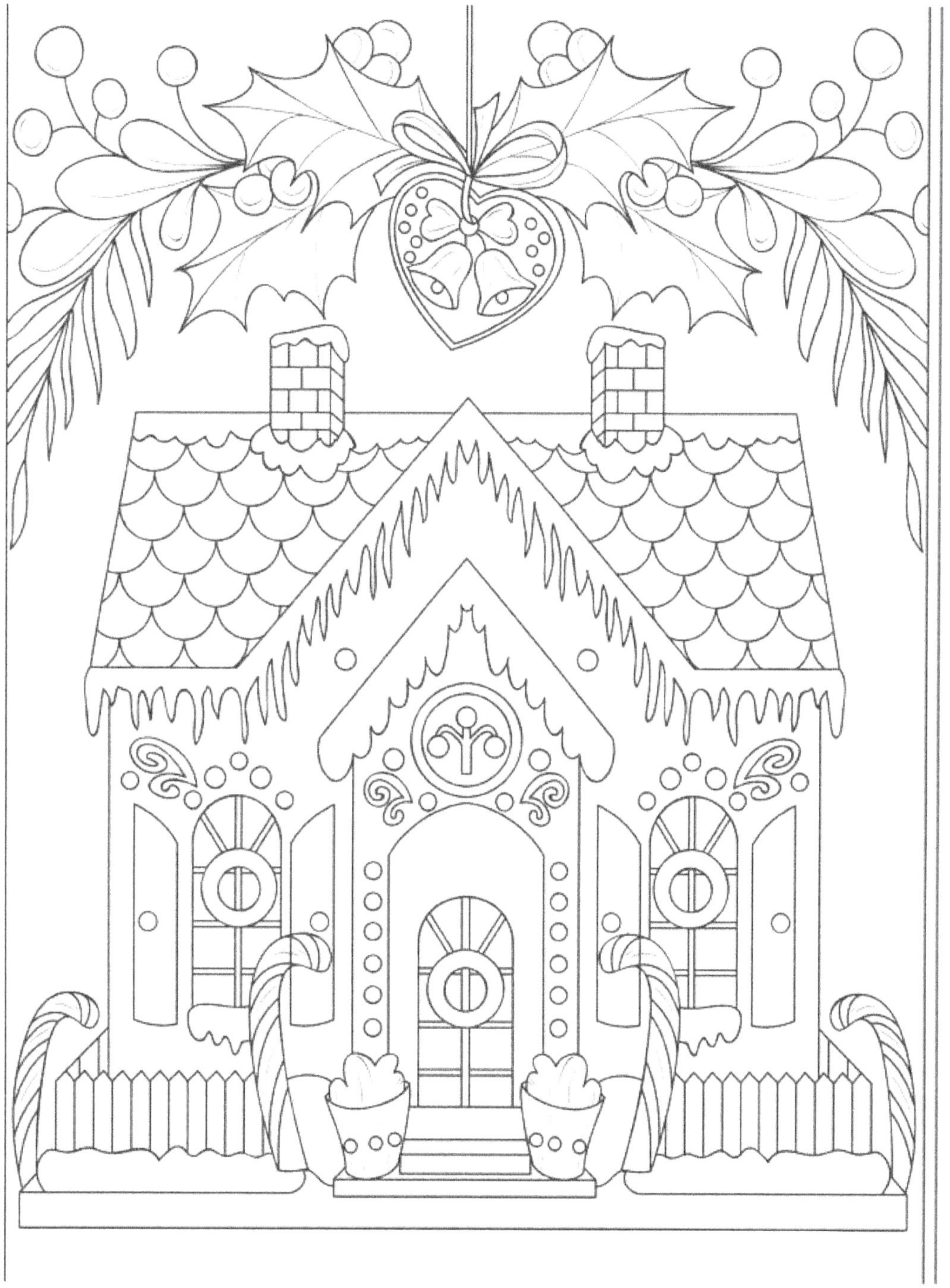

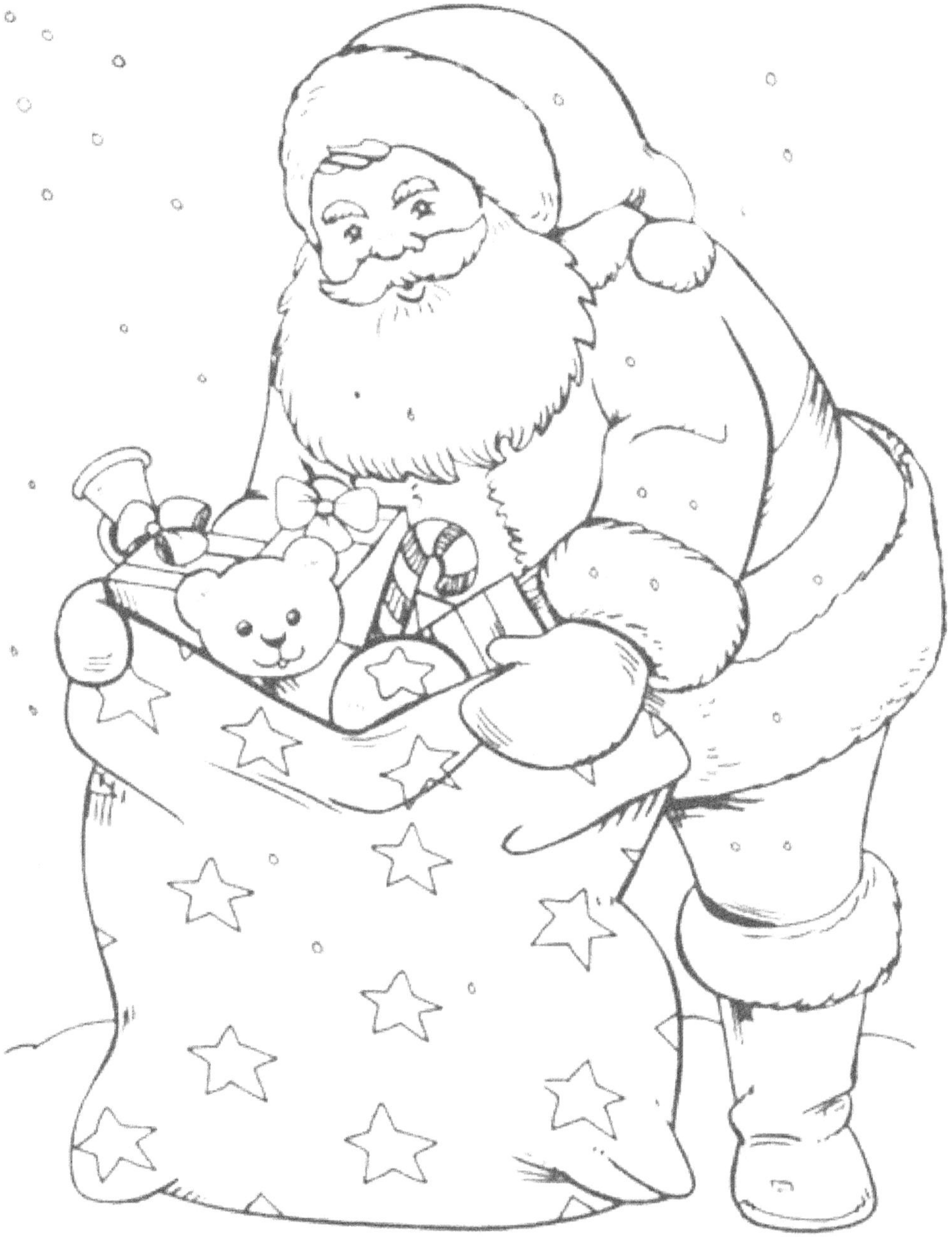

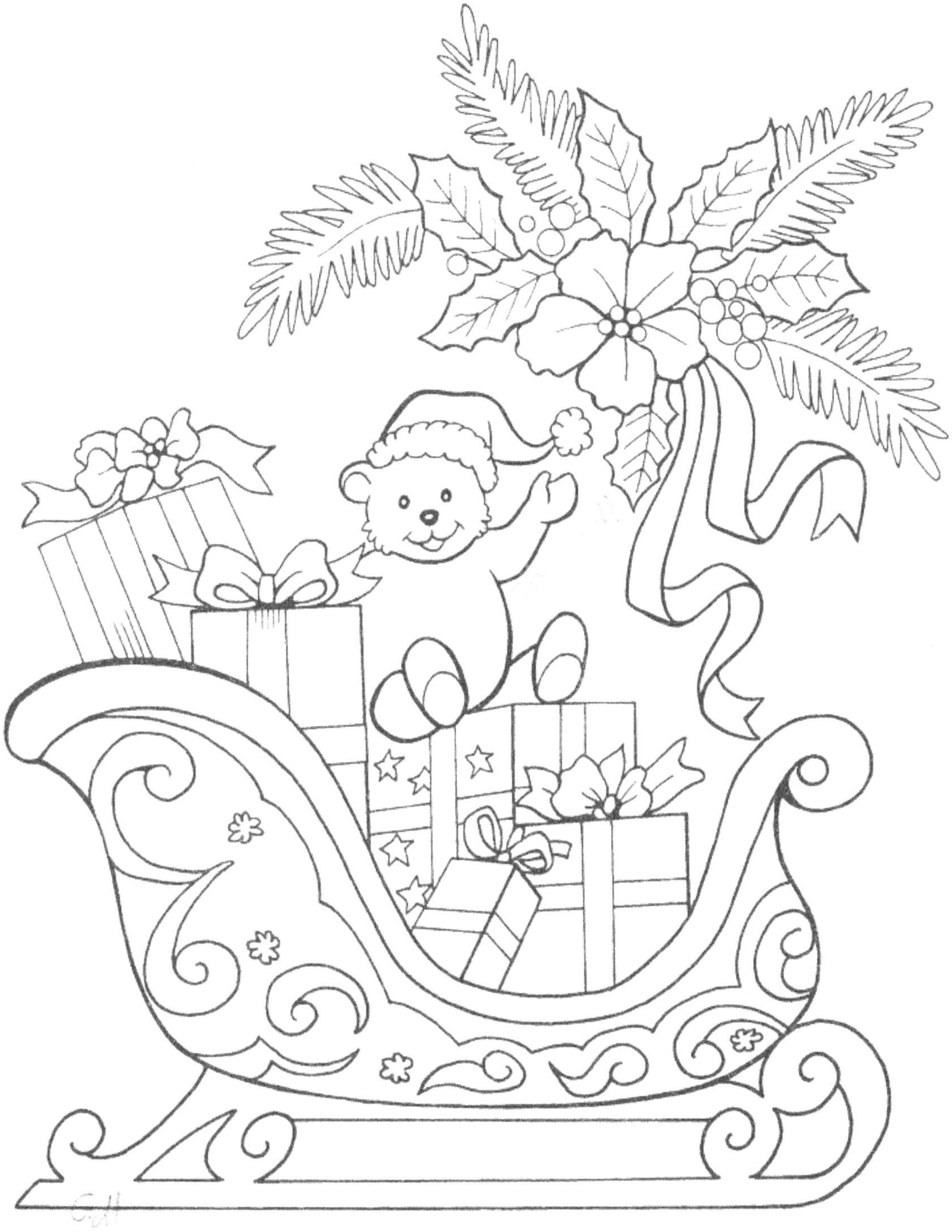

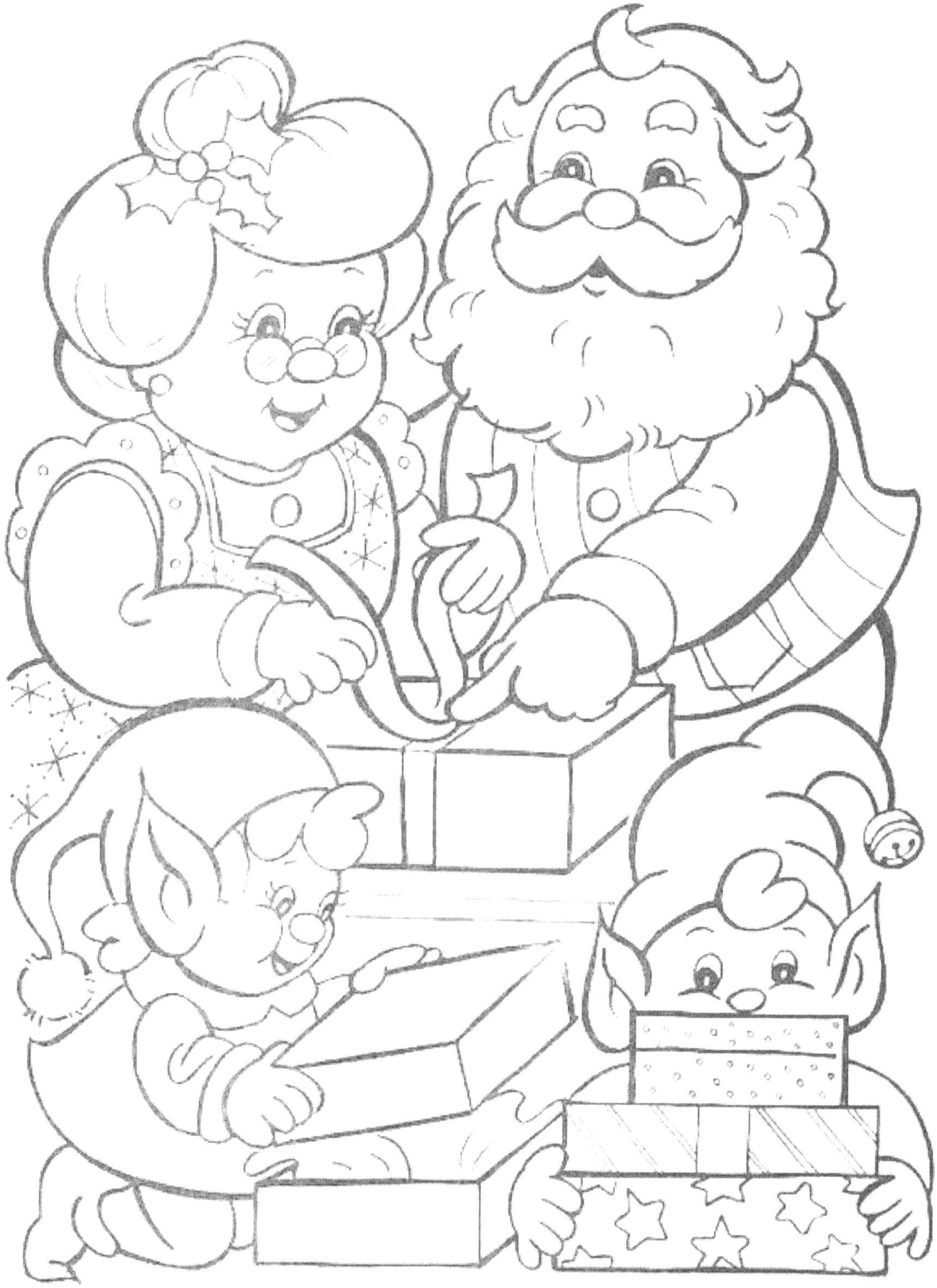

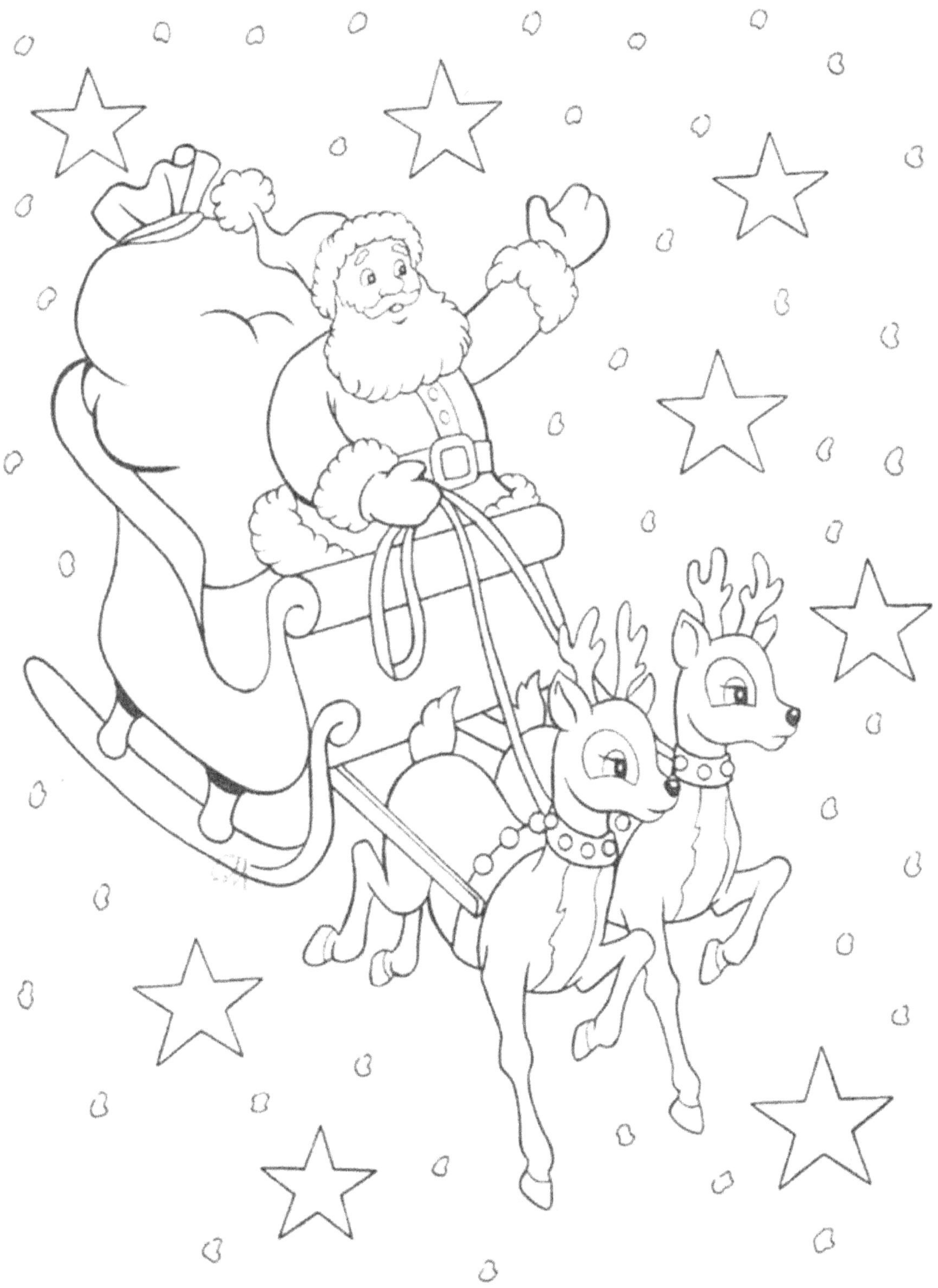

www.ingramcontent.com/pod-product-compliance
Lightning Source LLC
Chambersburg PA
CBHW080444220526
45465CB00007B/2757
9798366118460